Meditations for Mothers

Other Books by Elisa Morgan

Meditations for Mothers

MOMENTS

WITH GOD AMIDST

A BUSY NEST

Elisa Morgan

MOTHERS OF
M♥PS.
PRESCHOOLERS

ZondervanPublishingHouse
Grand Rapids, Michigan

A Division of HarperCollinsPublishers

Meditations for Mothers
Copyright © 1999 by Elisa Morgan

Requests for information should be addressed to:

📖 ZondervanPublishingHouse
Grand Rapids, Michigan 49530

Library of Congress Cataloging-in-Publication Data

Morgan, Elisa, 1955–
    Meditations for mothers : moments with God amidst a busy nest / Elisa
Morgan.
      p.   cm.
    ISBN 0-310-22654-6 (hc)
    1. Mothers—Prayer-books and devotions—English. 2. Motherhood—
Religious aspects—Christianity—Meditations. I. Title.
BV4847.M67   1999
242'.6431—dc21   98-32032
                                                       CIP

This edition printed on acid-free paper and meets the American National
Standards Institute Z39.48 standard.

Published in association with the literary agency of Alive Communications,
Inc., 1465 Kelly Johnson Blvd., Suite #320, Colorado Springs, CO 80920.

Interior art by Tammy Kutsuma Irvine
Interior design by Sherri L. Hoffman

Printed in the United States of America

99 00 01 02 03 04 05 /❖ DC/ 10 9 8 7 6 5 4 3 2 1

To Munna

Thank you for loving birds
and for directing my gaze
to follow yours in so much of life

Contents

Acknowledgments

Thanks to all those at Zondervan who believed in my "featherbrained" idea for this book. Special thanks to Sandy Vander Zicht and Rachel Boers, along with Jody Langley. You helped capture what I felt God had placed in my heart.

Thanks, as well, to Rick Christian, of Alive Communications, for his continued belief in me and in MOPS International.

I am also grateful, as always, for the nest from which I function in my daily life. Evan, Eva, and Ethan—I love you! Fly free and strong from the foundation of my love.

May God use the words contained in this devotional to nurture many mother birds in their roles as nest-builders.

*R*EST IS NOT IDLENESS, AND TO LIE SOMETIMES ON THE GRASS UNDER THE TREES ON A SUMMER'S DAY LISTENING TO THE MUR-MUR OF WATER, OR WATCHING THE CLOUDS FLOAT ACROSS THE SKY, IS BY NO MEANS A WASTE OF TIME.   —*SIR T. LUBBOCK*

Introduction
Longing for Time with God

*S*hortly after we were married, Evan and I lived in a cozy lit-tle ranch-style house. My favorite part of the house was the kitchen—the kitchen window to be exact. In those days, before children, I often spent time at that kitchen window with God, gazing out at petunias in summer and golden aspen in fall. Unhurried and uninterrupted, these times with God fed my soul.

The spring of my daughter's birth brought the highlight view. While washing dishes one day, I looked up to find a bird building a nest on the roof beam of our covered patio. Twig after twig, branch after branch, she flew away and back until her messy makings revealed a cuplike wreath of safety. Home.

Over the next few weeks, I watched her hunker down over her eggs, leaving only for the briefest moments. She received visits from another sparrow—Daddy, I presumed. One day, scrawny heads popped up over the edge of the nest and, with open-mouthed demands, welcomed themselves into the world. For weeks I'd climb up on my kitchen counter, watch the birds, and enjoy God's creation.

We have since moved from that house. Today the view from my kitchen sink has changed. As I wash dishes, I watch handstands and somersaults, not birds and nature. Instead of golden aspens, I gawk at the TV. I sort through my mental to-do list and often find prayer left untouched at the end of the day.

Children have changed my freedom to spend time with God. Where once I had easy access to him, now noise and busyness and, well, children stand in my way.

I suspect most moms share my struggle. Caught between the demands of sports activities, homework, church programs, and a desire to provide decent meals and family time, most of us have precious little left for God. When's the last time you prayed without falling asleep? or journaled about God's work in your life? or read your Bible without interruption?

In Psalm 84:1–2, the psalmist writes of a similar plight:

How lovely is your dwelling place,
O LORD Almighty!
My soul yearns, even faints,
for the courts of the LORD;
my heart and my flesh cry out
for the living God.

In this pilgrimage psalm, written to be sung by those traveling to the temple to make restitution for their sins and to worship God, the psalmist writes of a longing of the heart for God. Because the Old Testament required a high priest to make sacrifices for specific sins, worshipers longed for the temple and the priest so they could obtain forgiveness and access to God.

Verse three goes on,

Even the sparrow has found a home,
and the swallow a nest for herself,
where she may have her young—
a place near your altar,
O LORD Almighty, my King and my God.

The psalmist envies the birds who nest daily in the temple and therefore enjoy a daily presence in God's dwelling.

Mothers are among today's faint of heart who long for a time with God. While we no longer need a high priest to provide the forgiveness Christ offers through his death on the cross, we still long for the "temple" of time with God. Parent pilgrims grow weary and cry out for God.

This book is about taking a tip from the swallow in the psalm. She built her nest in a place near God's altar. She lived where God lived. We moms who long for God don't have to go somewhere special to find him. We can spend time with God when we build a nest near him and then enjoy everyday moments in it with him.

The following meditations are written to help you find moments with God in the midst of a busy nest. They're short and simple, so you can fit them into your day. At the same time, their messages are designed to stir your thoughts during these days and offer you calm and perspective in your daily life. Accompanying each meditation are questions to ponder called "Feather Your Nest," as well as a prayer for the day.

It's true that we can see God's presence in our lives through many illustrations from creation: the changing weather, animals, the mountains, the ocean. Somehow the pictures of a nest and nesting uniquely capture the challenges mothers face in raising and feeding their young while in desperate need of food themselves.

It's been over six years since we moved into our present house. My son, Ethan, just built a birdhouse with his dad. When it came time to hang it up, there was no question as to where it should go: on the deck outside the breakfast room window. If I raise the blinds, stand on tiptoe, and crane my neck just right, I can see it from the kitchen sink.

PART ONE

Nesting Instinct

RESTING IN THE VERY PRESENCE OF GOD

Hope is the thing with feathers
That perches in the soul,
And sings the tune without the words,
And never stops at all . . .
—EMILY DICKINSON

Bird Fact

BIRDS ARE AMONG THE WORLD'S MOST SKILLFUL
NEST BUILDERS. FEW OTHER CREATURES EXHIBIT
SUCH A VARIETY OF ARCHITECTURE OR MATERIALS.

ALEXANDER WETMORE,
SONG AND GARDEN BIRDS OF NORTH AMERICA

*F*OXES HAVE HOLES AND BIRDS OF THE AIR HAVE
NESTS, BUT THE SON OF MAN HAS NO PLACE TO LAY HIS
HEAD.   —*MATTHEW 8:20*

When You Need a Rest

*J*ust when we're finally ready to lay our weary heads down
on our pillows at night, there comes a request for another
glass of water or money for the field trip, or "Puuuuuhhh-
lleeeezzzz, Mom, my shirt *has* to be clean for school tomorrow." One midnight when my son, Ethan, was about six, he
appeared at the side of my bed and awakened me with a question about sex—and how people "do it." I muttered a simplis-
tic reply, but sleep came very slowly after that.

It seems our sleep is constantly interrupted by someone
else's need! We're nudged awake by a baby's muffled cry, a
stuffed animal lobbed across our pillow, or an early-morning
plea for cereal.

Jesus understands our exhaustion. He didn't even have a
home of his own during the draining days of his ministry. The
Bible conveys event after event where Jesus was "up early in the
morning" or confronted by the diseased of "the whole town."
Following Jesus' example in our mothering can, indeed, be costly,
and the currency is often our much-needed sleep. Unlike Jesus,
we have a place to lay our heads. We just don't have any time.

Jesus not only understands our weariness, he offers a solution by contrasting his own lack of home with the fact that even birds have nests. In order to survive and thrive in these days of mothering, we need to build a home in God and time with him in it.

This is a hard task isn't it? Evidently, it's hard even for the birds. Naturalists tell us that our earth is quickly losing habitats for birds. Nesting spots are vital to the continuation of the species, so environmentalists fight to protect them.

Unfortunately, Sweet Mom, no one is going to protect and provide such a spot for us! Building a home with God is an undertaking we must choose for ourselves. A ten-minute reading of a favorite Psalm while our child is napping. Quiet moments of prayer in the car on the road from daycare to work. Suds-filled bathtimes late at night where we wash away the strain by reviewing all God has done in and through us that day. Nesting spots are moments when we intentionally build refreshment into our days where we can rest in the presence of God.

Following Jesus in our everyday lives may mean that we are up before the sun and asleep long after others in our households, but it doesn't mean that we have no rest at all.

Feather Your Nest

1. Do you identify with the need to find time with God?

2. Is there some way in which you've been expecting someone else to do this for you?

3. How can you find moments with God for yourself?

Prayer

Dear God, help me understand that while you had no place to lay your head, I can always "lay my head down" in my relationship with you. In you, I can build a nest of rest for myself. Show me, today, where such a "nest moment" is and help me to rest in it when I see it.

Bird Fact

Propagation is work. Real work. How a bird manages to charm a mate, design and construct a nest, incubate eggs, feed hatchlings incessantly, and defend its territory, seems an exhaustive, if not impossible feat.

Maryjo Koch, *Bird Egg Feather Nest*

BLESSED ARE THE POOR IN SPIRIT, FOR THEIRS IS THE KINGDOM OF HEAVEN. —*Matthew 5:3*

Admit Your Need

friend of mine herded four children (five to fifteen years old) about while her husband traveled for work. A long day with unending demands sapped every ounce of good intentions she'd aimed at being a "good mom" that day. In desperation, she grabbed the first harmless item she saw, and launched a Lunchable at her youngest, hollering, "Get your act together!" After dissolving in tears, she and her children laughed at the preposterous "weapon" she'd used to defend herself against her own neediness.

Such a response within ourselves surprises us at first. From our days before children (B.C.), we look ahead to imagine rocking sweet-smelling, contented newborns who coo at our approach and sleep upon command. Reality is an adjustment. Round-the-clock feedings, sacrificed personal time, long-abandoned date nights, Legos on the living room table. Where we once pictured ourselves gliding through the days of mothering, the everyday truth is that there's not quite enough of us to meet the needs under our noses. Suddenly we face a kind of

23

poverty in the mothering department as we discover we have nothing left.

Birds, too, struggle with the feat of parenting. Some baby birds need to be fed as often as every few minutes. That's quite a job! But while baby birds are "conceived," raised, and out of the nest in a matter of weeks, human children are much more demanding in their need for long-term commitment. Especially in the early years, their dependency seems to string out for years with requests that we cut their meat, tie their shoes, and get their chewing gum out of their hair!

Perhaps no vocation as much as mothering so continually points out what we lack as humans. Are you aware of your need? More often than not, we women prefer the illusion of meeting needs to having them. Jesus directs otherwise in Matthew 5:3. What he means here is that those of us who are able to admit and embrace our inadequacies and our need for God are *blessed*. Until we can see that we need God, we can't let him near. Until we understand what we can't do or be, we can't grasp who he can be in our lives.

Mothering is exhausting. Yes, it is fun and fulfilling and deeply meaningful. But it is sapping. When we admit our need for a rest, we're halfway home to help. Then comes the challenge of getting in the nest to rest.

Feather Your Nest

1. What is your most typical pattern for handling a need once you recognize it? Do you deny it? wallow in it? force it on someone else?

2. How might God want to help you with the need you're facing today?

Prayer

Dear God, I am needy. Help me to see this fact as a blessing, since it can point me to you and away from my habit of self-sufficiency. Help me to embrace this need, rather than deny it—and then to give it to you to meet.

Bird Fact

RED-WINGED BLACKBIRDS BUILD NESTS AROUND CATTAIL STALKS FROM LATE APRIL TO EARLY JULY. THE FEMALE MAY USE SWAMP MILKWEED STRIPS WOUND AROUND THE STALKS TO MAKE A CRADLE TO HANG HER NEST IN.

MEL BORING, *BIRDS, NESTS AND EGGS*

*H*E TENDS HIS FLOCK LIKE A SHEPHERD: HE GATH-
ERS THE LAMBS IN HIS ARMS AND CARRIES THEM CLOSE
TO HIS HEART; HE GENTLY LEADS THOSE THAT HAVE
YOUNG.   —*ISAIAH 40:11*

Close to His Heart

*W*here can we build our nest of rest, Mom? Surely there
are as many varieties of moms as there are species of
birds. But we can all find a home close to God's heart.

Birds build nests in amazing places. Some birds are finicky
and fret until they find *just* the spot. Others are "nest anywhere"
birds, hunkering down into an old hat abandoned in a barn,
stuffing themselves into a tin can in a field, or hiding beneath
potted plant leaves on a kitchen windowsill. Those who study
birds tell us that there are four basic nest locations:

- In cavities: Carved into another container, these nests
  are often found in tree holes, nooks of buildings, and
  birdhouses
- In the open: These structures are open to the sky and
  are typically cup shaped
- On the ground: Shallow and depressed into the ground,
  these are "open cups"
- Underground: These underground dwellings are actually hollowed out with tunnels and sometimes have very
  elaborate entrances

27

Using the metaphor of sheep and a shepherd, Isaiah describes how God guides those with young. Isaiah 40:11 focuses on God's calling his people out of captivity in Babylon and home to himself—out of a life separated from him and into a relationship of stability and security, close to his heart.

Close to his heart. Take your twigs, Mom. Gather your leaves and fly right up to the very heart of God. That's the best nesting spot for us, no matter what our bent as moms. When it's ten at night, and you've been up since five, and you have three more loads to wash and a stack of bills to pay, you need a nest close to God's heart. When you climb the stairs during what you thought was nap time to discover your eighteen-month-old has baptized his crib with his messy diaper, you need a nest of rest close to God's heart. When you're racing from baseball games to committee meetings to dental appointments, you need a nest where you can rest your heart close to God's.

Close to his heart. That's where he says he'll put us, we who have young. I don't know about you, but I can't think of a better place for a nest of rest.

Feather Your Nest

1. Where are you most likely to find God? In busyness or quiet? What most feeds your soul?

2. How might you adjust your nesting instinct to build a nest closer to God's heart?

Prayer

Dear God, help my heart beat more in sync with yours, that I might desire to live closer to your heart today.

Bird Fact

After bathing, the bird retires to a safe place to preen. Wetting the feathers before preening helps the spread of preen oil. Most birds have a preen gland at the base of the tail whose contents are smeared over the plumage . . . The oil does seem to keep the feathers from becoming brittle, and it has antibacterial and fungicidal properties.

Robert Burton, in
Treasury of North American Birdlore

*Y*OUR DWELLING PLACE IS SECURE, YOUR NEST IS SET IN A ROCK.
—*NUMBERS 24:21*

Safe Nests

A king once offered a reward to the artist in his kingdom who best depicted the concept of peace on canvas. Myriads of murals were submitted, but the one the king chose illustrated a mother bird building her nest in a rock behind a waterfall. While the bird wove her reeds into a nest, water cascaded powerfully before her. Unfazed by the roar about her, she knew she was in the right spot, and so she nested peacefully.

When *I* think of building a nest, my mind pictures secure sprigs nestled in a sturdy spruce. When the wind howls, I rush to add another twig. When the rains pelt, I flutter forth with more leaves to patch a leak. I view my role as mother to be one of guaranteeing safety and peace for my nest and all who dwell within. It's all up to me.

Hmmm. Could it be that safety and peace come not so much with my flitting and fluttering, but with where I choose to build my nest in the first place?

Safe nests are those built in the Rock of a God who cares about every daily moment. The Rock—God—is there when the baby spits up on our shoulder just as we were ready to finally walk out the door. The Rock is there when our husband

31

completely misses our cue for a break. He is there when a friend brags on about her brilliant child just when we're really worried about the progress of our own. And he is there when a job falls through after round four in the interview process.

In these stormy moments when the wind buffets our nest, we can trust our safety only if we've built our nest firmly in God. What keeps us safe is not our expert weaving or our selection of the most perfect nest-building materials. Safe nests are those that are built in the Rock who is God.

Feather Your Nest

1. What do you think really keeps you safe?

2. What risk might you take today to discover the safe nest you can have in a relationship with God?

Prayer

Dear God, I am fearful of really trusting you with _____. Help me to give this need to you, knowing it is you, alone, who can really provide safety. Show me today how to build my nest in you, the Rock.

Bird Fact

THE HUMMINGBIRD WEIGHS NO MORE THAN A PENNY. IT IS ONLY ABOUT 3-1/2 INCHES LONG AND BATHES ON A FLOWER LEAF WITH DEWDROP WATER. . . . [YET] IT CAN OUT-FLY ANY BIRD AND FLY IN ANY DIRECTION, EVEN BACKWARD AND UPSIDE-DOWN AT THE SAME TIME. AND HUMMINGBIRDS ARE FAST FLYERS. THEIR AVERAGE SPEED IS 30 MPH, BUT THEY HAVE BEEN CLOCKED UP TO 50 MPH.

MEL BORING, *BIRDS, NESTS AND EGGS*

*COME TO ME, ALL YOU WHO ARE WEARY AND BUR-
DENED, AND I WILL GIVE YOU REST.* —*Matthew 11:28*

Losing Your Stress

A few years back I sat on my then-ten-year-old's bed and leaked out my worry over whether I should undertake another book project. My schedule was packed. There wasn't enough of me to go around. While I knew my child couldn't "fix" my dilemma, I was so surrounded by it that it shadowed the very space between us.

"Eva," I pondered, "Do you think I should write another book?"

Her answer surprised me with its simplicity. "Do you *want* to write another book, Mom?"

The thought had never occurred to me. I was so lodged between the last commitment and the next that I hadn't taken even a second to consider what I *wanted* to do, only what I *could* still fit in my hours and minutes.

Ornithological illustrator Maryjo Koch reports that, in order to fly, birds need an extremely high metabolism. In fact, "a human being with the metabolic rate comparable to that of a hummingbird's would burst into flames." Yet this seems to be my specialty: overcommitting and facing the resulting stress. I squeeze in two more errands when I'm already late and the kids are crabby. I undertake a "feast" for company instead of a simple meal. I promise my children stay-up-late nights, forgetting I have an early commitment the next day. I say yes instead of no way too often—until I'm sizzling, risking spontaneous combustion.

Jesus speaks to moms like me (and you?) who are weary and burdened by the stresses of life, whether self-imposed or unavoidable. *Come.* One simple action is all that is needed. An entreaty. An invitation. *Come. Sit in a nest of rest near my altar. It's what I want for you.*

Whether hummingbird or swallow, a bird is gifted with a metabolism that is inhuman—so that it can fly. We are not birds, Mom. But we have been gifted with a metabolism that equips us to meet the needs around us—without bursting into flames.

Feather Your Nest

1. Where in your life are you saying yes when you should be saying no? To whom are you really saying yes, and why?

2. How do your wants match up with what God wants?

3. Do you hear Jesus' voice saying, *"Come,"* today? How will you respond?

Prayer

Dear God, help me to consider my own giftedness when I face commitments. Show me how to sift through what I want and what you want. And when you say, "Come," make my feet quick to move.

PART TWO

Nest-building

LIVING WITH GOD IN THE DAY-TO-DAY

*Despite overall similarities, each nest identifies
its maker as surely as an artist's signature.*
—MARYJO KOCH

Bird Fact

KILLDEERS ARE VERY SNEAKY NESTERS. THEIR NEST IS HARDLY EVEN A NEST. IT IS JUST A SHALLOW HOLLOW ON THE GROUND WITH STONES AND A LITTLE GRASS AROUND IT.

MEL BORING, *BIRDS, NESTS AND EGGS*

OH LORD, YOU HAVE SEARCHED ME AND YOU KNOW ME.

—*PSALM 139:1*

Just the Way You Are

Are you a "nest anywhere" mother? Are you happy to plunk down amidst boxes from last Christmas and build a blanket fort? Do piles of unfinished laundry sit without accusation in the next room while you focus on a school project with your oldest? Good for you!

But maybe you're not so sure. Perhaps you struggle to get situated in your "anywhere nest." Your neighbor's nests are all "just so." They talk about how they craft their nests and what next addition they're planning. Not a twig or a string is out of place in their perfect nest, and you eye your own hodgepodge mixture of feathers and straw with uncertainty. Will your "nest anywhere" inclinations harm your children? Are you somehow missing what is more important?

Many species of birds don't really care where they build their nest or what it looks like. A nest is a nest. Whether it be in a tree, under a roof beam, teardrop shaped, or hung like a sack in a high branch—it really doesn't matter. They are as dedicated to nest-building as other birds. They are just as conscientious as other mothers. They, too, lay their eggs, hatch their

41

young, feed hungry mouths, and watch healthy fledglings fly away. Still, for them, function triumphs over aesthetics. These are known as nest anywhere birds.

In Psalm 139:1–4, 13–14, God reminds us that he is intimately familiar with who we are as mothers because he is the one who made us:

> O LORD, you have searched me
> and you know me.
> You know when I sit and when I rise;
> you perceive my thoughts from afar.
> You discern my going out and my lying down;
> you are familiar with all my ways.
> Before a word is on my tongue
> you know it completely, O LORD. . . .
> For you created my inmost being;
> you knit me together in my mother's womb.
> I praise you because I am fearfully and
> wonderfully made.

Whether you are a "nest anywhere" bird or a more persnickety type, allow room in your life for who God made you to be. While all of us can grow in true discipline and organization, moms tend to overemphasize the value of these qualities. It's not the house, it's the home that creates a nurturing nest for children to grow.

Feather Your Nest

1. Do you believe that there is a "right" and a "wrong" way to make a home? Where did you get this perception? Should you reexamine it?

2. Is God reshaping your view of your home? What do you need more of in your home? What do you need less of?

Prayer

Dear God, indeed, I am fearfully and wonderfully made—just as I am—because you made me. Help me to see myself as you do. To embrace what is good and adjust what needs improvement. Make my home a reflection of who you have made me to be, and help me to dwell in it securely.

Bird Fact

FOR THE MALE EMPEROR PENGUIN INCUBATION IS A LONE ORDEAL. THROUGH THE BLACK ANTARCTIC WINTER, WHEN TEMPERATURES PLUNGE TO 70 DEGREES BELOW ZERO, HE NESTLES THE SINGLE EGG ON HIS FEET BENEATH A BELLY FLAP. FOR TWO MONTHS HE NEVER LEAVES THE EGG TO FEED, BUT LIVES OFF HIS BODY FAT. IF HE MOVED AWAY, THE EGG WOULD INSTANTLY FREEZE.

ALEXANDER WETMORE,
SONG AND GARDEN BIRDS OF NORTH AMERICA

WHATEVER YOU DO, WORK AT IT WITH ALL YOUR
HEART, AS WORKING FOR THE LORD, NOT FOR MEN . . .
IT IS THE LORD CHRIST YOU ARE SERVING.

—*COLOSSIANS 3:23–24*

No Regrets

The tailorbird sews—literally stitches—her nest out of leaves. Don't believe me? It's true! She usually starts in a potted plant, just inches off the ground. Selecting either a single large leaf or a cluster of smaller ones, she carefully pierces an equal number of holes on each leaf edge with her sharp, pointed bill. Next, gathering spider silk or strands of cotton, she actually stitches back and forth through the holes, joining leaf seams together as if lacing a tennis shoe.

The tip-top of the pouch is left open for an entrance. Through this shoot, she stuffs down grasses and leaves for softness. Whether her well-stitched nest is tucked into a houseplant on a windowsill or hangs from a park tree, the tailorbird rests secure, her young growing accustomed to the rocking of the breeze even before they are born.

Our nest is the home we build to live in, raising our young in the presence of God. How seriously do you take this home-building stuff?

Paul's words in Colossians 3:23–24 were once intended for slaves, but today they apply to all who are working for a distant reward. Who really notices what we do as moms? The T-shirts folded in thirds, tomato-sauce spot removed. The empty twelve-pack of Coke replaced by a new one. The alarm clock set for the teen who forgot to. The hair appointment missed in order to attend a school conference. The midnight temperature check for a sick child.

Poke, stitch. Poke, stitch. Poke, stitch. Stuff. Stuff. Stuff. No one may notice, Mom, but like the little tailorbird, when you stitch security into your home, you hem your offspring in to handle the breezes of life.

Feather Your Nest

1. Look back over the past few days and spot a time when you felt completely undervalued as a mom. Now recall your goal: *working for the Lord*. How does this change your attitude? Your feelings?

2. Is there someplace in your mothering where you've ignored your job of poking and stitching? Where do you need to "sew up" a spot in your nest?

Prayer

Dear God, lace the thread through my beak, I pray. I am tired of poking and stitching. So often it seems that it doesn't matter anymore. Help me believe that the investment of my efforts today will pay off in the future for my children—and for myself. I don't want to look back with regrets for what I could have done, but didn't.

Bird Fact

NEST BUILDING TAKES PLACE MOST FREQUENTLY IN THE MORNING. THE MALE USUALLY GUARDS THE BIRDHOUSE WHILE THE FEMALE MAKES TRIPS TO GATHER NESTING MATERIAL, OR HE MAY FOLLOW HER AROUND.

DONALD AND LILLIAN STOKES,
THE COMPLETE BIRDHOUSE BOOK

"MARTHA, MARTHA," THE LORD ANSWERED, "YOU
ARE WORRIED AND UPSET ABOUT MANY THINGS, BUT
ONLY ONE THING IS NEEDED." —LUKE 10:41–42

Knowing When to Stop

House wrens distinguish themselves from other nest builders by a unique habit of overbuilding. Their custom is that whatever place they select—large, small, or in-between—they must fill it completely before it feels "finished." Say they find a tiny spot under an eave. Fine. The nest is built to fit the spot and no more. But if they discover a knothole that opens to a wide expanse, they will build and build and build, adding stick and wad and bulk until the nest is massive. It seems they have no concept of what is enough. If there is space, it must be occupied. In some couples, the male actually invests himself in building several nests and then allows the female to select one, letting the others go to waste.

I feel as if I'm looking in the mirror when I read the above description. That's me. If I give away a piece of clothing, I quickly replace it with something new. If there's a free spot on my calendar, I rush to pen something into it. If nap-time silence fills my home, I turn on the TV. If I invite guests over for a celebration, I make not one dish but nine.

In Luke 10:38–41, we read the story of Mary and her sister Martha. (Why don't we ever identify them as Martha and her sister Mary?) Jesus has come to visit their home. Both women are excited, but each expresses her welcome in quite a different manner. Mary sits down, focuses her attention on her guest, and listens. She *is*. Martha mixes a meal for Jesus. She *does*.

Now, Jesus needed to eat, and someone had to mix the meal. But Martha didn't stop with one course. Instead, she fixed up a feast with preparations that took her solely into the world of *doing* and out of the sphere of *being* with her guest. Her actions actually removed her from his presence.

So what about you, Mom? Are you like the house wren and Martha, lost in the art of *doing* just because there is more to be done? When is enough enough? When a guest comes to your home, will you keep building—or invite him in to sit with you in the space you already have?

Feather Your Nest

1. Why do you think it is easier for some of us to *do, do, do* instead of *be*?

2. Where in your life do you need to stop *doing* and choose instead to *be*?

Prayer

Dear God, when you come knocking today, help me to first hear your voice and then to resist the urge to move into action in response and instead to simply join your presence.

Bird Fact

TODAY'S BIRD SCAVENGES IMAGINATIVELY, PLUCKING

RAW MATERIALS NOT ONLY FROM THE ENVIRONMENT

BUT FROM THE . . . FRUITS OF ITS OWN BODY AS WELL.

MARYJO KOCH, *BIRD EGG FEATHER NEST*

Put Yourself into Your Mothering

Are there days, Mom, when your mothering becomes completely "othering"? There are seasons when we seem to be required to invest even *our bodies* in the vocation of mothering. Pregnancy. Nursing. Middle-of-the-night feedings. Muddled brains from processing math we once understood. Missing meals to care for someone sick. Tired knees from praying for a gone-astray child.

Radio speaker, author, and mother Mary Whelchel is enchanted with eagles and with the spiritual lessons we can see in their nest-building practices. Listening to her describe the finishing touches on an eagle's nest, I was pierced by the mother eagle's investment in her home. It seems that once she builds the eight-foot by ten-foot monstrous nest (which has been said to look like a bonfire waiting for a match), she then softens the nest by plucking down from her own chest. Adding a fluffy bit here and there, like pillows accenting a color scheme in a living

53

room, the mother eagle completes her nest with an offering of her own body.

But does putting ourselves into our mothering require only self-denial and pain? Is that what God desires of us? I don't think so. In the passage above, Paul is discussing the overall care for our bodies in this life, and that *offering* our bodies means nurturing ourselves as much as sacrificing ourselves. In order to be able to invest daily in the lives of our loved ones, we must also nurture our bodies with rest—and our souls with time with God—so that we will have something to offer.

There will be days to pluck the feathers from our chests to soften the nest where we raise our young. And then there will be days when we, too, must cuddle up in the down to rest, caring for our own bodies and souls.

Feather Your Nest

1. Have their been times when you have "plucked the down from your own chest" to soften your nest for your loved ones? What were those moments like?

2. What can you do to nurture your body while you sacrifice it?

Prayer

Dear God, help me understand the balance of sacrificing myself while still nurturing myself. Show me today where I can build nurture into my life—alongside the sacrifice—for you.

Bird Fact

FOR NESTING, [PILEATED WOODPECKERS] CHOOSE A TALL, BRANCHLESS STUB IN DENSE FOREST WELL WITHIN THE LEAFY CANOPY OF LIVE TREES. THEY RETURN TO THE SAME VICINITY, OFTEN TO THE SAME TREE, YEAR AFTER YEAR. BUT THE COUPLE MAKES A NEW APARTMENT EACH YEAR. SOMETIMES A FAVORITE TREE IS RIDDLED WITH THEIR OVAL ENTRANCES.

ALEXANDER WETMORE,
SONG AND GARDEN BIRDS OF NORTH AMERICA

I WILL REMEMBER THE DEEDS OF THE LORD; YES, I WILL
REMEMBER YOUR MIRACLES OF LONG AGO. I WILL MEDI-
TATE ON ALL YOUR WORKS AND CONSIDER ALL YOUR
MIGHTY DEEDS. —*PSALM 77:11–12*

Layering God's Lessons in Your Life

I can remember when I thought I'd never be able to handle
one after-school activity. It seemed I'd crack under the stress
of merely considering Girl Scouts *and* swimming lessons. But
layer by layer, I figured out how to fit my kids' schedules into
mine, how to navigate between commitments, and even how
to ask another mom to trade off driving. Looking back, I mar-
vel that God truly intervened, teaching me one step at a time.
When I bump into new challenges today, I draw strength by
looking back at how far I've come.

It's so easy to think that today is all there is. Stuck in a spot
where we are slaves to potty training, or carpooling, or meal-
making, or simply the agenda of others, it's tough to keep the
truthful perspective that today is simply *part* of life, a slice of
the bigger pie of existence.

The hummingbird's nest symbolizes a way to keep perspective intact. Hummingbirds build layers of fern leaves,

mosses, and grasses into their nests, all secured with spider silk—lots of spider silk. (One nest was found to have an estimated 15,000 *miles* of spider silk!) The first year the nest is built, it is only about three inches in height, but each year the hummingbirds return to the same nest, adding on so that it becomes taller and taller.

God encourages us to layer the lessons of our lives like the hummingbird layers the years of her nest. He longs for us to not limit his love and interaction in our lives to a single experience or two but to *remember* his work day after day, month after month, year after year, and so to gain perspective.

Layer your nest, Mom. Today isn't all that life is made of. Look back to God's faithfulness yesterday and the day before. Remember his actions in your life and in the lives of those you love.

Feather Your Nest

1. Looking back, what can you remember about God's faithfulness to you as a child? as a teen? as a young adult? What message has God layered in the nest of your relationship in him?

2. Today is not all of life but it is a part of life. How is God demonstrating his care for you in this season? What can you do to layer the lessons of today into your life?

Prayer

Dear God, thank you for your faithfulness over the years in my life. Today, remind me that this is a layer of life, not all of it. Help me to remember your actions and to gain perspective for living.

PART THREE

Birds of a Feather

ASKING FOR HELP FROM OTHERS

*A friend knows the song in my heart
and sings it to me when my memory fails.*
—*ANONYMOUS*

Bird Fact

INCUBATING BIRDS DEVELOP BROOD PATCHES—
AREAS ON THE ABDOMEN THAT ARE BARE OF FEATH-
ERS. HERE NETWORKS OF FINE BLOOD VESSELS LIE
CLOSE TO THE SURFACE. THESE DISTRIBUTE BODY HEAT
AND KEEP [THE EGGS] AT THEIR NORMAL INCUBATING
TEMPERATURE—ABOUT 93 DEGREES.

ALEXANDER WETMORE,
SONG AND GARDEN BIRDS OF NORTH AMERICA

I LIE AWAKE; I HAVE BECOME LIKE A BIRD ALONE ON
A ROOF. —*PSALM 102:7*

When You're Lonely

*M*othering can be a lonely vocation. Even if we thrive on
these busy days, there are moments when we look up
from our tasks at the sink or our taxiing in the car, or our never-
ending "to-do" list, and we long for the companionship of
another. A kindred spirit. A soul who understands our soul. An ear
who will take in our thoughts and allow us to complete a sen-
tence without interruption. This need is not the same as "aloneness," where we long for five minutes of peace. No, this is the
ache of loneliness, where we long for five minutes of connection.

We're lonely in our little nests. What is the answer for us?
In the gathering of women's prayers entitled *Soul Weavings*,
Catherine Brandt points to a solution. She prays,

> Lord, I'm lonely, a sparrow alone on the housetop.
> Yes, I know you are right here,
> But I crave human companionship. Is that wrong, Lord?
> Someone to sit awhile, to look at me and see me,
> to listen and really hear.
> Someone to say, "You count with me. I care about you."
> Lord Jesus, you visited the lonely world.

You brought love and comfort to the solitary.
Turn me about. Let me reach out.
Is there someone I can listen to?
Someone in need of my companionship and your love?

Some birds—like cliff swallows—actually build their nests in great communal gatherings. If this is not your style or your reality, you can meet your need for companionship in other ways. Invite someone into your home. Fly over to the neighbor next door. Stop off at the home of another on your way back to your own. Attend to the plight of someone who is lonely like you, and you'll ease your aloneness by linking your life to another.

Feather Your Nest

1. How often do you struggle with being "a bird alone on a roof"?

2. Can you distinguish between lonely times and alone times? How are they different?

3. Who do you know who might struggle with the separation of loneliness? How can you help?

Prayer

Dear God, I am lonely. I can tell this is not a need to just be alone. I miss contact with another. I need companionship. Please show me today who in my world might be struggling as I am, who I can reach out to— that you might reach out to me through her as well.

Bird Fact

NESTING TERRITORIES VARY IN SIZE. BIRDS THAT GATHER IN COLONIES . . . MAY DEFEND ONLY THE FEW SQUARE INCHES THAT THEIR NESTS OCCUPY. . . . BUT MOST SONGBIRDS STAKE OUT CLAIMS FROM A FEW SQUARE YARDS TO SEVERAL ACRES IN EXTENT AND DEFEND THEM WITH BATTLES ROYAL.

ALEXANDER WETMORE,
SONG AND GARDEN BIRDS OF NORTH AMERICA

DO NOT JUDGE, AND YOU WILL NOT BE JUDGED. DO
NOT CONDEMN, AND YOU WILL NOT BE CONDEMNED.

—*LUKE 6:37*

Mommy Wars

I sat on the window seat in my room at a conference cen-
ter. It was early morning, and I was preparing for the day—
nesting if you will. Suddenly a cache of birds bulleted their way
to an eye-level tree. They tore leaves from its branches with their
beaks, then raced off to another tree across the street. Then they
were back, this time pecking at each other instead of the tree.
They seemed to fight over each leaf. *How odd,* I thought. *There's
an entire tree full of leaves and they're fighting over one.*

As I've grown more familiar with the ways of birds, I've
come to understand that this tussling for territory is part of a
bird's nest-building instinct. Most birds simply won't tolerate
competition for space from a bird of the same species. Another
variety is welcome, but not a bird of the same feather. And once
boundary lines are settled, birds protect them desperately, even
creating "sidewalks" in the air from tree to tree for nest
approach and departure.

While this fighting might be an acceptable pattern in
birds, I can't help but see a sad parallel in us as moms. We look

67

over in the grocery line at the mom who says yes to her child's whines for checkout candy and sigh, "She's ruining him." We hesitate to venture into the doctor's office for fear our child will be exposed to "their" children's germs. We fence our homes about with the security of same-race, same-class, same-belief friends in order to insure our child's—and our own—comfort. We cluck under our breath at the working woman who wrestles her child from her car while still clad in her business attire, or we tsk, tsk toward the stay-at-home mom dressed in sweats and a ponytail.

Their choices are not ours—but are they wrong?

We need each other too much to give in to this temptation. Rather than separating ourselves from one another because we think differently on certain positions or ways of living, perhaps it's time we embrace our common desire to be the best mothers we can be and to reach out to each other to help make that possible.

Whether another mom is "right" or "wrong" or just differs from us, there is great wisdom in Jesus' admonition here. We need each other too much to fight.

Feather Your Nest

1. In an honest moment with yourself, consider whether your views on certain ways of living are the only right positions, or whether others could actually see things differently and still be "right" before God.

2. Is there someone you exclude from your life because she is different from you? How would God have you adjust your attitude and your actions to include her?

Prayer

Dear God, help me not to disqualify other mothers from friendship. Reveal my need for those who are different from me to complement my offerings as a woman and as a mother.

Bird Fact

A MALE HUMMINGBIRD REQUIRES NECTAR FROM 1,000 FUCHSIA BLOSSOMS TO MAINTAIN ITS METABOLISM FOR A SINGLE DAY.

MARYJO KOCH, *BIRD EGG FEATHER NEST*

Love Birds

Evan and I were married for five years before we became parents. Our patterns were well-established and comfortable. We enjoyed our couple time, but we'd also built private time into our relationship. "My time" was coffee with my best friend. Evan's was golf. It wasn't until after children that I noticed that while "my time" took me away for two hours, Evan's took him away for six! His outing left me with the baby *much longer* than mine left him with her. Suddenly I began to resent golf—big time.

Some birds have a relationship of practical love with their partner. The male often chooses the territory, while the female chooses the nesting site. The female may build the nest while the male stands guard. When it comes to feeding young, males often feed their partner so that she can feed their babies. Partners in parenting, these mates are involved together in the process from the moment the nest is built until the fledglings fly away.

Most of us long for such a relationship within the nests where we raise our young. We count the hours our husband is away and mentally log them. "If only he would help around the house!" we moan. Or notice our needs. Or show an interest in us.

Marriage is one of the most trying environments for the growth of love. In the familiarity of the home, we learn revealing truths about ourselves and about our spouses. Like the fact that our husbands don't always seem to know how to parent like we do. Or the reality that we'd really rather serve our children than serve our husbands because there's less of a power struggle with our children.

Here's the truth: marriages need regular feedings in order to grow in love. Marriage may be a tough place to demonstrate love, but it also may be the most important. Truly, when we love best the ones we're with the most, we grow in love, and so do they.

Okay, so maybe your husband doesn't stand guard over your home the way you desire. Perhaps he doesn't even select the territory. And maybe he doesn't know where to begin to feed you so that you can feed your young. What is there in him for you to honor? to respect? to enjoy? to admire? to cherish? Start there. Focus on feeding your husband the nurture he needs, and then watch your mating begin to grow to partnering.

Feather Your Nest

1. Take out a piece of paper and list five characteristics you admire in your husband. Now write him a note detailing each and leave it under his pillow.

2. Reconsider what you are doing to grow yourself into a more committed and loving partner. Are you focused more on your children than on your husband? Why do you think this is the case? How can you adjust your priorities?

Prayer

Thank you, God, for my husband. Reveal to me why I love him and grow my love for him stronger today.

Bird Fact

THE MALE RED-WINGED BLACKBIRD LOOKS LIKE AN ARMY GENERAL. WITH RED AND YELLOW SHOULDER PATCHES, THE BLACKBIRD SEEMS TO SCREECH OUT ORDERS: "OAKA-LEE!" THE FEMALE LOOKS DRESSED LIKE A SOLDIER, IN DULL BROWNS AND WHITE ON HER WINGS AND CHEST. SHE SPEAKS WITH SHORTER, SOFTER WHISTLES, "TEE-TEE-TEE-TEE."

MEL BORING, *BIRDS, NESTS AND EGGS*

SUBMIT TO ONE ANOTHER OUT OF REVERENCE FOR
CHRIST.   —*EPHESIANS 5:21*

Is Your Way the Only Way?

*E*van and I differ in how we play with our children. We
always have. When they were little, I cooed. I built blanket forts and dragged armloads of books inside, where we read
and giggled. Evan's style was to walk in the door, grab a toddler, and throw her up in the air with a "Whoooooop!"

We each also handle household issues in our own way.
Evan loves spotless counters and beds that are made up. I do
too, but I forget. I'm more relentless about the volume of the
TV and the brushing of teeth.

And when I'm away from home, Evan's version of parenting looks different from mine. He feeds the kids whenever
and whatever—none of it from the refrigerator. They watch
more TV. They stay up later.

Such differences in parenting can be cause for conflict, if
we let them. Many times I've bristled with Evan's choice. He
didn't let the kids go next door to play when they could have.
He made them stick close by him at the store instead of explor-
ing. His choice wasn't *my choice*. And it bugged me.

While not all species of birds parent as couples, most do. Perhaps they split up the chores of nest-building and egg incubation, but most share the tasks of feeding and training. Watching them from your window or in the park, you'll see a weaving of their offerings. He selects the nest site. She approves it and brings moss in her beak for the first layer. He adds a twig and a feather. She sits on the eggs and he flies to and fro to feed her, since she cannot leave the nest. She gives. He gives. No correction from her to him. Just reception of his offering for the nest they share together.

Paul writes of submitting or *yielding* to one another in his letter to the Ephesians. When I apply that to my life, I think of making room in *my way* for Evan's. You see, when we value only *our way* and view our husband's method as wrong, we'll miss out on the help he gives. And so will our children.

Feather Your Nest

1. In what spots do you struggle to validate another's offering?

2. How can you relinquish your insistence on *your way* to make room for another's?

Prayer

Dear God, yield my way to the ways of others. Most of all, dear Jesus, yield my way to yours and to what you desire most in my days and in the days of my family.

Bird Fact

INDIVIDUAL LEARNING BY BIRDS IS SOMETIMES REMARKABLE. FOR EXAMPLE, IN ENGLAND, TITMICE OF VARIOUS SPECIES LEARNED TO OPEN MILK BOTTLES LEFT IN THE EARLY MORNING ON DOORSTEPS AND TO REACH DOWN INTO THE BOTTLE AND DRINK THE MILK. WITHIN 30 YEARS THE HABIT HAD SPREAD AMONG THESE BIRDS TO MANY PARTS OF ENGLAND, POSSIBLY THROUGH THOSE WATCHING AND IMITATING OTHERS OF THEIR KIND.

JOHN TERRES,
IN *TREASURY OF NORTH AMERICAN BIRDLORE*

Learn from Other Mothers

Most of what I know about mothering I learned. I didn't know it before I was a mom. Some I learned on my own, in the push-pull moments of meeting needs, of not having enough of me to meet needs, and in somehow getting through.

Some of my most meaningful mothering lessons have come from other mothers. Over lunches. On the phone. Through conversations in parking lots while waiting for kids. When I'm with other moms, my eyes and ears are always working, taking in what they do with their children, hunting for hints on how I can raise my own. I'm learning to embrace how much other mothers can teach me about mothering if I simply watch and listen.

It hasn't always been this way for me. I've had to *learn to learn*, if you know what I mean. For a long time, I assumed that other moms knew all about how to mother and that they had no questions or insecurities. In my mind, I was the only one *pretending* to know how to mother. Slowly, over time and long cups of coffee with safe friends, I've come to understand that most of us are still in-process. Some are further than others, but we're all still on the way to where we want to be.

Amazing as it is, birds learn—and then pass their lessons on through the generations. Watching each other and imitating, they've integrated skills of feeding, pulling strings to open doors, building better and better nests year after year. Without embarrassment or agenda, they observe one another and integrate what they find in their own worlds.

What a relief it would be if we could realize this mom-to-mom opportunity for learning early on in our mothering careers! Drop the facade! Release those fears of being found out! Embrace each other's efforts and see what works! Resist the urge to mother alone. Get together with other mothers and free yourself to learn. You'll be a better mom for it.

Feather Your Nest

1. Can you admit what you don't know about mothering?

2. If you had three questions to ask another mom about mothering, what would they be?

3. To whom can you reach out, get to know, and learn from in your mothering?

Prayer

Dear God, please put other mothers in my life and help me learn from them. Free me from the feeling that I have to have all the answers. Release me to learn what I don't know yet.

PART FOUR

Bird Seed

BEING FED BY GOD

My Lord and God, the words of Your Spirit are laden with delights. As often as I hear them, my soul seems to absorb them and they enter the heart of my body like the most delicious food, bringing unbounded joy and unspeakable comfort. After hearing Your words, I remain both satisfied and hungry—satisfied, for I desire nothing else; but hungry, for I crave more of Your words.

—ST. BRIDGET

Bird Fact

SONGBIRDS ARE BLIND, PRACTICALLY NAKED, AND UTTERLY HELPLESS WHEN THEY HATCH. . . . THE INFANT'S TOTAL EXISTENCE IS A STEADY ROUND OF GAPING FOR FOOD, SWALLOWING WHAT IS PUMPED DOWN THE GULLET, DIGESTING, DEFECATING, AND SLEEPING.

ALEXANDER WETMORE,
SONG AND GARDEN BIRDS OF NORTH AMERICA

OPEN YOUR MOUTH WIDE AND I WILL FILL IT.

—*PSALM 81:10*

Are You Hungry for God?

I peered into the cupboard for dinner makings only to find a very small selection of possibilities. When I opened the freezer, vapor curled from the empty shelves. A bag of stale tortillas stared at me from the refrigerator, daring me to be creative.

And then my son, Ethan, stubbornly refused to do his homework. Period. There was no negotiation. Nothing worked. Not pleading, threatening, or—to my humiliation—crying.

There seem to be so many afternoons like this. Nothing to feed my children. No answers for meeting their needs. Little left over for myself, either.

I separated myself from my son, went to my room, got on my knees, and prayed. "What now, God?" I didn't hear God tell me what to do, but I did regain my composure. And when I returned to the kitchen table, I found my son, head bent over his homework.

There are times I long for God so deeply that I can *taste* him. It's like I'm starving for a few bites of perspective. Or truth. Or faith. Or hope. Know what I mean? Looking back at the above instance, I believe I simply needed a few bites of

God's presence in my afternoon. He wanted to feed me so I'd have enough to feed my children.

In many bird species, the father bird feeds the mother, who is "stuck" on the nest incubating the eggs. His devotion continues when the young are hatched and he brings the mother food to feed them. What a picture of God, tenderly feeding us as moms! He pries our lips open and offers a few bites of perspective from the Bible. He pushes us gently to our knees, where we can dine on his presence. He sets out snacks of trials and joys so that we feel our hunger for his provision.

Open your mouth, Mom. God wants to feed you so that you can feed your brood.

Feather Your Nest

1. Are you hungry for God? What do you most desire of him?

2. Right now, pray the prayer, and ask God to meet this need.

Prayer

Dear God, I open my mouth, my mind, my soul to you. I am starving. Feed me, I pray, that I might feed the hungry in my home and in my world.

Bird Fact

VISION IS THE BIRD'S MOST HIGHLY DEVELOPED SENSE.
UNLIKE MOST ANIMALS, THEY SEE IN COLOR. NEARLY
ALL BIRDS FIND THEIR FOOD BY SIGHT, AND MANY
MUST BE VISUALLY ALERT TO AVOID PREDATORS.

ROGER F. PASQUIER,
IN *TREASURY OF NORTH AMERICAN BIRDLORE*

S THE DEER PANTS FOR STREAMS OF WATER, SO MY SOUL PANTS FOR YOU, O GOD. MY SOUL THIRSTS FOR GOD, FOR THE LIVING GOD. WHEN CAN I GO AND MEET WITH GOD? —PSALM 42:1–2

Developing a Taste for God

When my children were babies, neither of them particularly cared for water. Drinking it, that is. Oh they loved *playing* in it. They merrily splashed and kicked through their bathtimes. They plunged eager arms up to the shoulders into suds-filled sinks. They dragged hoses through flower beds to sprinkle each other in the backyard.

But drinking water was something they disdained. They disliked the taste, or according to them, the lack of taste. "It's just *water!*" they'd complain. Even as hiccuping infants, they'd push away the prescribed cure of a bottle of water. Only recently, as sports freaks, have my children finally learned to love drinking water and recognize its taste of health.

It seems that baby birds have a similar repugnance for drinking water. The one difference is that their dislike is rooted in the fact that, early in their lives, drinking water is dangerous. As babies, they receive water through their food. They develop the ability to drink water very gradually as they mature. Small birds can die if forcibly fed water.

When the psalmist writes of panting for the presence of God like a deer pants for water, it is both the tasting and the processing of God's presence to which he is referring. Growing in our relationship with God means salivating for the taste of who he is as well as applying his ways in the everyday moments of our days.

Mom, it seems that some of us need to develop a *taste* for God's presence, while others must gain the ability to *process* it. But all of us need him. Which struggle belongs to you: the dislike of what is good for you, or the inability to take it in? Do you thirst for God and how he wants to meet your needs? Does the offering of his truth trill out of your lips as if you don't know how to swallow?

Help comes for us all when we determine to take small sips. Read all of Psalm 42 today. Turn the TV off for ten minutes and pray that God will give you a stronger desire for spending time with him. Ask a friend to pray for your lack of interest in God. Both the taste and the processing of God's ways takes time and commitment to develop . . . a sip at a time.

Feather Your Nest

1. Can you remember a time in your past when you were more "thirsty" for God? What has happened since then?

2. Is it possible that you've substituted some other "drink" for God's water in your life? When you are really honest with yourself, is this substitute satisfying your thirst?

Prayer

Dear God, my tongue is parched. Please bring me a drop of your presence and teach me to drink again.

Bird Fact

THE INSIDE OF A BABY SONGBIRD'S MOUTH IS
BRIGHT-COLORED——RED, ORANGE, OR YELLOW. . . .
HIS BRIGHT MOUTH MAKES A PROMINENT TARGET
FOR THE PARENT BIRDS. THE SIGHT OF IT SETS OFF A
RESPONSE IN THEM——A STRONG DESIRE TO CRAM
FOOD INTO THIS GLEAMING CAVITY.

ALEXANDER WETMORE,
SONG AND GARDEN BIRDS OF NORTH AMERICA

LATE IN THE AFTERNOON THE TWELVE CAME TO HIM
AND SAID, "SEND THE CROWD AWAY SO THEY CAN GO TO
THE SURROUNDING VILLAGES AND COUNTRYSIDE AND
FIND FOOD AND LODGING, BECAUSE WE ARE IN A
REMOTE PLACE HERE." HE REPLIED, "YOU GIVE THEM
SOMETHING TO EAT."   —LUKE 9:12–13

When There's Not Enough of You to Go Around

"I'm hungry!"

I looked at my son with disbelief. Not ten minutes before, I had placed the final eating utensil in the dishwasher, sighed with completion, and moved my tired body from the kitchen to the family room. Dinner was done. Where had he put the plate of spaghetti that had just been before him? I remembered it full. I remembered it empty. I thought I saw him shoveling forkfuls into his mouth. Maybe I had been hallucinating.

"I'm hungry!"

These are the first words I hear in the morning and often the last ones I hear at night. An hour after breakfast. Thirty seconds after they're in the door from school. And just before bedtime when the humongous meal of the evening has suddenly vanished from my children's bodies.

If kids had their way, they'd eat nonstop from dawn until dusk. Birds do, you know. Barn swallows eat about once a minute. A hummingbird must consume its weight in nectar daily, feeding every ten to fifteen minutes from dawn to dusk. And baby birds—well, they demand food constantly, creating a full-time job for both parents with little, if any, break.

It's not just physical food that kids crave. They also want attention, time, presence, security, and love—all in heaping helpings offered around the clock. This command-feeding aspect of mothering is intimidating. Even in my best moments as a mother, I simply cannot meet every need my children have. There isn't enough of me.

We're like the disciples on the mountain that day, facing tens of thousands of growling stomachs. Like them, we turn to God and go, "Your problem!" What amazes me is how often he responds to us as he did to the disciples when he said, "You give them something to eat."

And then it happens. We go to the cupboards of our souls and ponder what we have to serve. We hand over our ideas for a school-play costume, and God turns it into an outfit. We intercede into a squabble between friends, and God patches a wound. We reach out with our own lessons from making a mistake, and God meets a need for forgiveness.

"You give them something to eat," Jesus says. And then he takes what we have in our hands and multiplies it to meet the need before us.

Feather Your Nest

1. Think back on a time when God took what you had in your hands (in your "soul" cupboard) and multiplied it to meet the need of your child or your husband.

2. Look into your heart. Are there exceptions to this multiplication rule? Is there any need God can't meet if you submit yourself to his working?

Prayer

Dear God, sometimes it seems that the needs before me are completely beyond me. And then you say, "You feed them." Help me not to run in fear at such a moment but to put what I have in your hands and then to wait for you to use me to meet the need before me.

Bird Fact

PROBABLY NO BIRD IN THE WORLD FLIES SO FAR TO FIND THE NEEDED FOOD AS THE WANDERING ALBATROSS. BANDS ATTACHED TO THEIR LEGS PROVE THAT THESE ADULTS WILL TRAVEL UP TO TWENTY-FIVE HUNDRED MILES FROM THEIR NESTS TO FIND FOOD FOR THEIR SLOW-GROWING, INFREQUENTLY FED, SINGLE CHICKS.

HELEN G. CRUICKSHANK,
IN *TREASURY OF NORTH AMERICAN BIRDLORE*

THEREFORE I TELL YOU, DO NOT WORRY ABOUT YOUR LIFE. . . . LOOK AT THE BIRDS OF THE AIR; THEY DO NOT SOW OR REAP OR STORE AWAY IN BARNS, AND YET YOUR HEAVENLY FATHER FEEDS THEM. ARE YOU NOT MUCH MORE VALUABLE THAN THEY? —MATTHEW 6:25–26

Don't Worry

The rain fell in fat drops on my windshield. Oh no! Baseball practice would be cancelled and I was at least thirty minutes away. Ethan would be drenched. I turned at the corner and sped down what has always been a shortcut—until today. Brakelights greeted me with more frustration.

I fussed and fumed to the air—and to God—about how much I wanted to be a good mother and how good mothers were *always* on time to pick up their children and *never* left their children stranded in the rain where other mothers could see them abandoned and waiting. Turning down yet another neighborhood street, I found I'd entered a cul-de-sac and had no choice but to make a U-turn and nose myself back into the line of traffic. *Ethan's going to kill me. I'm such a lousy mother. He'll probably be abducted. Or catch pneumonia.*

For the remaining two miles of my trek, I was miserable. My heart pounded. My palms itched. My head throbbed. I was being a complete worrywart.

As I sped into the school parking lot, I peeled my eyes for any sign of Ethan. I dreaded seeing the coach with Ethan in his car, waiting for me and concluding that, with a mother like me, Ethan must be a brat and didn't deserve to play the next game. But as I careened to the curb, the coach was nowhere in sight. I realized that other mothers were waiting as well. With a glance at the dry pavement in the parking lot, it occurred to me that the rain hadn't hit this section of Denver. Twenty minutes later, practice finally over, Ethan headed to the car and plopped happily down beside me.

I had worried for nothing. God had fed my sparrow, protected him from a downpour, and placed him beside me in a warm car. I was still a good mother both for him and in front of the others who sat in their running cars.

Get the point? How much of our lives do we spend fretting over what never happens? Lots. And the rest of the time we worry over what doesn't matter a bit in the first place. Jesus makes a sane point that we who worry should take to heart. If he takes care of sparrows who aren't able to take care of themselves, he'll take care of us. If we let him.

Feather Your Nest

1. What do you worry about the most when it comes to your children? How realistic are your fears?

2. Is there a way in which your worrying might get in the way of God's working in your life?

Prayer

Dear God, please forgive me for worrying. I seem to think that if I take control of more in my life, my life will work better. Help me get out of your way so that you can work your ways into me and into those I love.

Bird Fact

MANY BIRDS HAVE A CROP—A COMPARTMENT IN

THE GULLET WHERE FOOD IS STORED.

ALEXANDER WETMORE,
SONG AND GARDEN BIRDS OF NORTH AMERICA

$\mathcal{M}$OSES SAID TO THEM, "IT IS THE BREAD THE LORD HAS GIVEN YOU TO EAT." . . . EACH ONE GATHERED AS MUCH AS HE NEEDED. THEN MOSES SAID TO THEM, "NO ONE IS TO KEEP ANY OF IT UNTIL MORNING." HOWEVER, SOME OF THEM PAID NO ATTENTION TO MOSES; THEY KEPT PART OF IT UNTIL MORNING, BUT IT WAS FULL OF MAGGOTS AND BEGAN TO SMELL.

—EXODUS 16:15, 18–20

God Has Something for You—Every Day!

When I know I'm going to be out and about for the day, I usually tuck a banana or a package of string cheese into my purse in case I get hungry and need a fix. On the days I forget, you don't want to be around me! In such moments I'm forced to grab whatever's within reach: York Peppermint Patties, Peanut M&Ms, cookies. My blood sugar goes nuts, my head throbs, and my patience evaporates. It's not pretty.

In much the same way, God has built into us the need for fresh, daily times with him. Grabbing whatever's handy or depending on a "meal" we had days ago just doesn't provide the spiritual nutrition necessary for our souls. Like the Israelites in the wilderness, when we try to store up God's provision from one day to another, lazily believing that it'll be enough or even doubting that he might have something new for us, our souls suffer.

Some birds are able to store food from day to day. The shrike hangs morsels on tree branches like a butcher store's slabs of meat in a locker, so that it has nutrition at its beak's tip in a pinch. But what works for the birds in this instance won't work for us. We moms need a daily dose of God's perspective, care, and hope. Without time with God—even if it's a few minutes grabbed here and there—we're forced to reach for whatever is convenient. Tabloid headlines. A friend's well-meaning but off-base belief. Last week's scrap from a devotional that might hold out some hope but dries up as we try to apply it to where we are today.

I know it's tough, but it's not impossible. Resist the urge to store up God's provision. Depend on him each day. When you get up in the morning, go to God in your mind and begin the day with him. When you run errands, imagine Jesus along with you in the passenger seat. When you go about your daily duties, ask his advice for the bumps you incur. When you retire after your day, reminisce with him about what you've learned and how his presence made a difference.

Tomorrow, do the same anew. God's nurture is unending. He wants to give you fresh food today and every day.

Feather Your Nest

1. Are there times when you feel that it's just too much trouble to think about God? Where do such feelings come from?

2. Sometimes we suffer through seasons where we experience more of God's absence than his presence. How can you endure these times and learn to discover him even when he seems gone from your days?

Prayer

Dear God, help me resist the temptation today to stuff something else into my soul as a substitute for you. Speak to me newly of your presence in my life.

PART FIVE

Songbirds

TALKING WITH GOD IN YOUR OWN SOUL LANGUAGE

Let us be like the bird, for a moment perched on a frail branch while he sings. He feels it bend, but he sings his song, for he knows that he has wings.

—VICTOR HUGO

Bird Fact

SONG SPARROWS HAVE BEEN HEARD SINGING ALMOST

CONSTANTLY FOR NINE HOURS A DAY——MORE THAN

2,000 SEPARATE SONGS!

ALEXANDER WETMORE,
SONG AND GARDEN BIRDS OF NORTH AMERICA

Put a Song in Your Heart

I can always tell if the birds are working on their nest outside my kitchen window by their songs in the early morning. Long before I can *see* them, I can *hear* their music. Sure enough, when I gently raise the blinds and sneak a peek outside, there is Mom tucked into her birdhouse hole and Dad watching guard on a branch of a nearby tree. While she sits and he flies and brings food, they sing.

I can't help but think of Snow White's, "*Whistle while you work. Deedle deet deet deet deet deet!*"

On occasion, the cheeriness is too much for me. I wonder what they have to be so *chirpy* about, and I walk back to my chores with disdain. But on other days, I pull up a chair, perch in observation, and lose myself in their happy antics. They are committed to each other, to their nest, and to the hopes of their brood. Not a bad lot in life, really. And I look back over my life with a greater appreciation.

107

Think with me for a minute here. While your days may be filled with too many Legos under your feet and not enough time alone, what do you have to sing about? If you had to come up with twenty items under the heading, "Thank you, God, for" could you? Put aside the things you would "die to have" and jot down a mental list of what you do have.

It kind of changes the old attitude, doesn't it? Now one more thing. Try a tune. Flip through your favorite songs about God and punch one into your own throat. You don't have to be an accomplished musician to hum a song of praise. Move it through your mind in the shower. Hum it quietly at the sink. Put words to it and belt it out in the car.

Give yourself something to sing about in your mind and with your voice, and when you've finished the second verse, you'll probably have a song in your heart.

Feather Your Nest

1. Just as it takes time to form a negative attitude, it takes time to work out of one. In what area of your life do you want to start focusing on what God gives more than what you lack?

2. How does God's presence in a negative situation change the situation for you?

Prayer

Dear God, sometimes I just don't feel grateful for all you have done. Somehow the spots of woundedness or emptiness overshadow your provision. Help me to keep the perspective of your presence and the difference it makes in my days.

Bird Fact

WHEN A SIMILAR (OR IDENTICAL) SONG IS SUNG BY A
MALE TO COMMUNICATE WITH ITS MATE AND SERVES
NO AGGRESSIVE OR ADVERTISING FUNCTIONS, IT IS
SOMETIMES DISTINGUISHED AS A "SIGNAL SONG."

CHRISTOPHER LEAHY,
IN *TREASURY OF NORTH AMERICAN BIRDLORE*

> *B*UT I CRY TO GOD, AND THE LORD SAVES ME. EVEN-
> ING, MORNING AND NOON I CRY OUT IN DISTRESS, AND
> HE HEARS MY VOICE.   —PSALM 55:16–17

God Hears Your Cries

There are times when we desperately just need someone to hear our voice. Like when your toddler creates a crayon mural on your dining room wall. Or when you've come to the end of a very trying day of carpooling to nineteen events for three children and you round the corner into your bedroom only to discover cat vomit on the carpet—and no one else in the family has stopped to clean it up.

In such moments, we send a strong signal in search of someone who will listen.

Bird songs mean many things. Often the chirping we hear is simply males singing territorially: "You're in my space! Beware!" Different from these sounds are the "signal songs," sung mate to mate. These communicate, "Listen to what I have to say right now—I need you to know!"

The psalmist writes of this same need in you and me: wanting to be heard. Often we turn toward our husband—or our desire for a husband—with this need. Evening, morning, and noon, we so very much want him to enter our world, to see what it's like, and to care. We don't really expect him to fix anything; we simply want to know that he knows. And that we're not alone.

So what do we do? A couple of things. First, we send a signal to our husband, asking for his ear. In a good moment (like a Saturday morning or a Sunday evening, when life isn't so rushed), we ask for regular time for him to listen. And then we gently clarify that our talking doesn't make him responsible for fixing. In these listening moments, we just want his ears.

Second, we send a signal to the other mate in our lives: God. While a husband can grow in his ability to meet our need for understanding, only God can provide understanding perfectly, *evening, morning, and noon.*

Get that? Evening? Morning? Noon? We can cry out and God will hear our voice. Sounds just about right for you and me, doesn't it? We send the signal, and he hears our cry.

Feather Your Nest

1. Have you ever tried to explain your need for understanding to your husband? Do you think you could try it now?

2. How can you learn to cry out to God, evening, morning, and noon?

Prayer

Dear God, it's me. I'm sending you a signal song. I need to know that I'm not alone. Please respond today.

Bird Fact

BIRDS THAT SING FROM EXPOSED PERCHES SING
SHORT BUT SWEET PHRASES, WHILE BIRDS IN LESS VUL-
NERABLE SPOTS OFTEN SING FOR MUCH LONGER PERI-
ODS OF TIME.

MARYJO KOCH, *BIRD EGG FEATHER NEST*

*T*HE BIRDS OF THE AIR NEST BY THE WATERS; THEY SING
AMONG THE BRANCHES.   —*PSALM 104:12*

Do You Have a Safe Spot to Sing?

*M*y favorite place to sing is in the car, driving fast, sunroof open, windows down, CD blaring, and *alone*. I have to confess that there have been many occasions when I've demanded that my children turn their music low on the way to baseball practice or piano lessons or Bible study, only to crank it up myself when I'm on my own again. I sing best to God and really go for it in moments like this.

You may be like me, or you may prefer the communal approach. You find your voice set free on Sunday morning, praise band pounding, hands in the air. Or maybe you hum most freely when the clothes dryer is purring in accompaniment and your children's heads are bent over homework.

We may differ in our preferences for how and where we perform it, but all of us have a song to sing: a song of worship to express to God.

An interesting fact about songbirds is that while they always sing, they sing most freely when they feel safe. Analyzing the various songs of birds, one expert reports that birds actually sing "emotional release" songs—spontaneous outbursts that are neither territorial nor communicative mate to mate. They are simply songs. And birds sing them most fully if they feel free and protected.

So where, Mom, is your safe spot to sing? Where can you find your place to emote to God? Identify it. Seek it out. And sing! You'll be better for it, and so will those who live around you.

Feather Your Nest

1. What kind of music helps you feel close to God? How can you make more time to hear it?

2. If you don't have a safe spot to sing, look around your world and consider how you could create one. In the shower? Using headphones? In the car . . . driving fast . . . windows open?

Prayer

Dear God, there are many ways I need to emote with you. Help me to find and use a safe spot to sing my songs to you.

Bird Fact

SOME BIRDS JUST CAN'T CARRY A TUNE. VULTURES,

FOR EXAMPLE, HAVE FEW OF THE "MUSIC MUSCLES"

THAT CONTROL THE SCOPE OF SONG.

MARYJO KOCH, *BIRD EGG FEATHER NEST*

> *I*N THE SAME WAY, THE SPIRIT HELPS US IN OUR WEAK-
> NESS. WE DO NOT KNOW WHAT WE OUGHT TO PRAY FOR,
> BUT THE SPIRIT HIMSELF INTERCEDES FOR US WITH
> GROANS THAT WORDS CANNOT EXPRESS.
>
> —*ROMANS 8:26*

Silent Songs

Sometimes our songs are inaudible. They have no tune. No words. They reverberate within our souls but find no escape in expression.

Our husband looks at us quizzically when we try to explain this phenomenon. Our children have no clue that we can even sing inside ourselves. Even our friends puzzle. They understand the existence of an internal song. They strain to hear our tune, but they can't make it out.

Not all birds are songbirds. Vultures, for example, are born without the equipment necessary to sing aloud. There are times when I relate more to this species of birds than I do to the noisy nest builders outside my window.

Paul writes of this silent song in Romans 8. He refers to it as a song of the spirit. When we don't know how to word our prayers, our needs, we can offer only inward groanings, which the Holy Spirit interprets for us.

I've sung such silent songs. At the death of my niece (age six), one hummed within me, unable to find a tune. During my mother's cancer journey, when I had no prayers left to pray, a silent song sang in my heart. I heard another—no, felt another—at my father's death. One has played over the keyboard of my mind during various stages as my children have matured, my marriage has changed, my friends have moved, my calling has clarified. Not necessarily negative nor positive, these songs are contemplative with lingering messages.

Can your heart sing these silent songs to God? When you have no words, no idea how to form a prayer, can you let your heart form one? Maybe no one else will ever really hear it, much less interpret its meaning. But God hears all our prayers, even the silent songs that have no words. And he answers, soul to soul, spirit to spirit, song to song, silence to silence.

Feather Your Nest

1. Listen. Can you recall a time in your life when you sang a silent song to God? How did he answer?

2. For whom are you singing silently today? your child? your husband? your mother or father? your friend?

Prayer

Dear God, oh, how much I need you to hear my silent song. Please, Holy Spirit, sing my prayer for me. I am tired. I have no words and no voice.

Bird Fact

ALMOST ALL BIRDS LIVE AND LOVE AND DIE BEHIND
THE BARS OF NATURE'S COMPULSIONS. THEY ARE
CAPTIVE IN CAGES OF THEIR OWN INSTINCTS, FROM
WHICH, WITH RARE EXCEPTIONS, THEY CANNOT——
AND HAVE NO DESIRE TO——ESCAPE.

JOHN AND JEAN GEORGE,
IN *TREASURY OF NORTH AMERICAN BIRDLORE*

> $\mathcal{B}$UT THE MAN WHO LOOKS INTENTLY INTO THE PER-
> FECT LAW THAT GIVES FREEDOM, AND CONTINUES TO DO
> THIS, NOT FORGETTING WHAT HE HAS HEARD, BUT
> DOING IT——HE WILL BE BLESSED IN WHAT HE DOES.
>
> —JAMES 1:25

Songs from a Bird Cage

$\mathcal{I}$n the days of mothering young children, we can feel as if nothing is happening in or around us. It's so easy to just give up, figuring that nobody notices what we do or who we are anyway. We can even view our homes and children as "prisons" of sorts, barring us from experience with the variety and freedom we once knew.

Madame Guyon was a French noblewoman who was arrested in 1688 and falsely accused of heresy, sorcery, and adultery by envious church officials. After her conviction, she spent ten years in prison on these trumped-up charges. Yet Madame Guyon learned to embrace her limits and to sing from within her cage of captivity, as revealed in this poem she composed:

> A little bird I am,
> Shut off from the fields of the air;
> And in my cage I sit and sing
> To Him who placed me there;
> Well pleased a prisoner to be
> Because, my God, it pleases Thee.

Naught have I else to do;
I sing the whole day long;
And He whom most I love to please,
Doth listen to my song;
He caught and bound my wandering wing,
But still He bends to hear me sing.

My cage confines me round;
Abroad I cannot fly;
But though my wing is closely bound,
My heart's at liberty;
My prison walls cannot control
The flight, the freedom of the soul.

Oh! It is good to soar
These bolts and bars above,
To Him whose purpose I adore,
Whose providence I love,
And in Thy mighty will to find
The joy, the freedom of the mind.

While our lives as moms in no way contain the struggles of such a prison, Madame Guyon's song gives melody to the sometimes unspoken and misunderstood struggles of the season of early mothering where the demands can *feel* like bars about us. Our children's needs for our time, our arms, our intervention, imprison us from our own desires to read a book, complete a phone conversation, or even just nap. In truth, the boundaries of our days set us free to focus where God has placed us in this moment, at this time, for this task. And with those limits clearly set, life is more freely lived.

Feather Your Nest

1. Do you sometimes view your mothering life as a cage? How can Madame Guyon's perspective help you "soar beyond the bars"?

2. How does understanding your boundaries today actually free you to live more fully within them?

Prayer

Dear God, thank you—yes, thank you—for the definitions about my days that focus my attention on mothering. The task is so great and grand and the responsibility so grave that I am learning to love the very limits that help me live more fully as a mom.

PART SIX

Thorns, Snares, and Storms

SURVIVING LIFE'S TOUGH SPOTS

*Faith is the bird that feels
the light when the dawn is still dark.*
—TAGORE

Bird Fact

SHE'S CALLED A HORNBILL BECAUSE SHE'S GOT A BEAK
AS BIG AS A HOLLOW LOG, AND ON TOP OF THAT BEAK,
A HORN. . . . IT COVERS THE WHOLE OF HER FACE, AND
IT STICKS OUT IN FRONT OF HER LIKE A SPADE——TWO
SPADES CLAPPED TOGETHER, A CANNON, A CRAG, A
PENINSULA.

WALT WANGERIN, *THE MANGER IS EMPTY*

Choosing Between Staying and Straying

*E*ver get the itch to fly the coop?

The hornbill dwells deep within the rain forests of Africa. Her name comes from her beak, a mammoth megaphone-shaped protrusion. Like many birds, she invests herself in the incubation and hatching of her young, dedicating herself to their best interest.

Except this species of bird goes further. She enters a hollow tree trunk, where her nest awaits, and then, with the help of her mate, seals the opening shut using mud and dung. Next, she commits herself to the impossibility of flight. She turns her murderous beak on her own body and plucks her feathers—not the down of her breast but the primary feathers of her wings. By this action, she removes her ability to fly.

Why? Because the sharp shafts of these strongest feathers might wound her hatchlings in the nest.

Hmmm. Could I do this? Would I? Have I done it already? Her example makes you think, doesn't it? On some days the urge to stray is so palpable that I consider getting in my car and never returning to the neediness of the nest. My youth yawns out at me, fast becoming a memory. I want to abandon my obligations and chase it back before it rounds the next corner and is gone, out of sight forever.

I want to stray. Instead, I stay. I sit on my nest with the hatchlings I love and pluck another flight feather. Unlike the hornbill, I know my feathers will grow back to serve me in another season. I will nurture the nubs to insure their return.

Feather Your Nest

1. How do you cope when you face the choice between staying and straying?

2. Are there flight feathers you must remove for this season? How can you nurture the nubs where they once were to insure their regrowth later in life?

Prayer

Dear God, I confess I'm afraid to pluck my wing feathers for fear they will never return. The choice to stay in the nest—with my focus on this season—seems so expensive right now. Help me fasten myself here, with confidence that tomorrow will come.

Bird Fact

WITH ONLY BEAK AND CLAWS (AND SOMETIMES THE HELP OF A PARTNER), THE BIRD CONSTRUCTS A SAFE AND STURDY CONTAINER FOR ITS EGGS, OFTEN USING THE CURVE OF ITS BODY TO MOLD THE PERFECT SHAPE.

MARYJO KOCH, *BIRD EGG FEATHER NEST*

O JERUSALEM, JERUSALEM, YOU WHO KILL THE
PROPHETS AND STONE THOSE SENT TO YOU, HOW OFTEN
I HAVE LONGED TO GATHER YOUR CHILDREN TOGETHER,
AS A HEN GATHERS HER CHICKS UNDER HER WINGS, BUT
YOU WERE NOT WILLING.   —MATTHEW 23:37

God Wants to Gather You Up

Several years ago, after a forest fire in Yellowstone National
Park, forest rangers began the grueling task of exploration
to assess the fire's damage. One ranger found a bird petrified in
ashes, perched like a statue on the ground at the base of a tree.

Saddened by the sight, he knocked the bird over with a
stick. Three tiny chicks scurried out from under their dead
mother's wing. This mother, knowing danger was imminent,
gathered her chicks under her own wings, giving her life to
save theirs.

I can't say that I've ever gone quite this far in my mothering commitment. I've lost sleep caring for a sick child. I've
intervened in disputes with schools, taking the brunt of criti-
cism. But I've not been called to give my life for my children
the way this bird gave hers for her chicks.

Perhaps that's not the only point to this story, though.
Reading it through again, I'm struck by another action, just as

powerful as the mother's sacrifice: the compliance of the chicks. They trusted her wings' coming over them in provision and protection. They submitted to her help.

Jesus bemoans Israel's unwillingness to receive him as their Messiah. I wonder how often he longs to gather me and you under the protection of his wings but we are unwilling to cooperate. "I'm okay." "I can do this on my own." "I'd rather do it my way." How often we pull away from the help God has for us! A friend offers to take the kids for a while, but we decline. An unexpected nap time stretches before us, yet we busy ourselves with work instead of rest.

When the fire comes, God longs to gather us under his wings, Mom. Will we let him?

Feather Your Nest

1. Has God reached out in the past to cover you with his wings? What has been your response?

2. What objections do you put up today as you rush to get out from under God's covering? When you compare your objection to his cover, how does your side hold up?

Prayer

Dear God, somehow I always seem to believe I'll be better off without you in charge, that I can handle things on my own. Please forgive me. Help me to see and face the danger of life without you so that I can choose, instead, life with you.

Bird Fact

RENESTINGS MAY OCCUR AFTER A SUCCESSFUL FIRST
BROOD, OR THEY MAY OCCUR IF THE FIRST ATTEMPT
IS UNSUCCESSFUL. MANY BIRDS KEEP TRYING TO
RAISE YOUNG THROUGHOUT A SEASON, EVEN AFTER
ONE OR TWO UNSUCCESSFUL ATTEMPTS.

DONALD AND LILLIAN STOKES,
THE COMPLETE BIRDHOUSE BOOK

> ARE NOT TWO SPARROWS SOLD FOR A PENNY? YET NOT
> ONE OF THEM WILL FALL TO THE GROUND APART FROM
> THE WILL OF YOUR FATHER.   —*MATTHEW 10:29*

When a Sparrow Falls to the Ground

Do you know how a mother eagle teaches her baby to fly? She nudges her little one out to the edge of the nest. There the baby sits, precariously on the edge, peering down at the yawning gap below him. Then comes the amazing part. She shoves him off the edge. He has no choice but to flap and flail helplessly. He weaves and dives, sputters and spurts, but does not fly. Just as he is sure that he will be dashed against the rocks, the mother swoops beneath her baby, catches him on her wings and returns him safely to the nest, where she repeats the process over and over until the flapping baby finally flies.

At first, this illustration may seem cruel. How can the mother eagle put her baby in such danger? He might lose his life before he ever takes his first flight from the nest! Yes, but learning to fly involves risk. And as difficult as it may be to observe a mother's tough love, the lesson is clear: The mother is just as involved in her baby's falling as she is in his flying.

Think about it. Your toddler takes her first wobbly steps across the family room floor, excitement bubbling from her heart, and you lean back, offering her yet another step of independence as she reaches for you. Your six-year-old confidently crosses the street to play at a neighbor's house, and you hide behind the living room curtains, out of his sight but keeping him in yours until he is safely through the front door.

When God says that no sparrow falls to the ground apart from his will, he means that he, too, is as involved in the falling as he is in the flying. He holds the desires of our hearts as his own because he is the one who created us with them. He opens his arms to receive us when we return after being disobedient. He extends his reach to the recesses, where we retreat away from him. And yes, he nudges us up to the edge of our own human limits and watches us as we fall past them into fresh understanding of our continuous need for him.

God is just as involved in our falling as he is in our flying, Mom. No matter how far or fast we fall, he will be there to catch us.

Feather Your Nest

1. Have you ever experienced the presence of God in your "falling" moments? What was it like?

2. Are there ways in which you could learn to "fly" in no other way than by "falling"? Why this is true?

Prayer

Dear God, the second I see the edge of the nest, I tend to panic, feeling that you are only in the nest and not beyond it. Help me to trust you as I fall in order to learn to fly.

Bird Fact

ONCE BOUNDARY LINES ARE SETTLED, THE FEELINGS OF THE BIRD TOWARD HIS TERRITORY MOUNT WITH THE PROGRESS OF HIS NEST, UNTIL HE SEEMS TO DO DESPERATE THINGS PARTICULARLY NEAR THE NEST SITE. FLYING AT THE WINDOWS AND THE SHINY GRILL-WORK OF AUTOMOBILES IS NOT BIRD HARA-KIRI. IT IS TERRITORY DEFENSE.

JOHN AND JEAN GEORGE,
IN *TREASURY OF NORTH AMERICAN BIRDLORE*

Free Yourself

Ethan and his friend James were in the backyard building
a fort. Another one. You know, the kind with a gazillion
blankets, safety pins, and every household possession I own put
to a use its creator never would have imagined. We were a half
hour away from the arrival of James' mom to pick him up. In
my mind, I stewed over making the boys clean up the mess or
letting them play until the last minute. Before I knew it, the
doorbell rang and Ethan's happy friend greeted his mom.

After James left, I remembered the backyard mess and
chided myself for my indecision. I'd let them get away with too
much. They'd never learn. What kind of mother was I, anyway?
Sighing, I ventured outside only to discover that, to my aston-
ishment, the mess was gone. The boys had spotlessly removed
every object—on their own. Wonders!

For much of my life I have been ensnared by the trap of
perfectionism. Breaking out of this trap leads me to face yet
another one: self-doubt. When I choose to let the little things
go, I condemn myself for not being perfect. This shouldn't be

surprising. Most counselors will tell you that breaking habits often leads to internal conflict because the new, perhaps healthier behavior is unfamiliar.

Where are you easily ensnared in your "mom" days? And how, like me, do you free yourself from one trap only to encounter another? Male robins are so fiercely territorial during breeding season that they often become their own worst enemies. One robin was spotted pecking away at his own reflection in the side window of a parked car. It seems he'd protected his turf well, but had turned on himself in the process!

Mom, there are very real temptations around us: impatience, worry, fear, the myth of insignificance in our role as mother, jealousy, negativity, perfectionism, doubt. Fighting these battles can lead us to new skirmishes with self-doubt and self-condemnation as we try to change old behavior to new. Maybe you need to risk the frustration of letting your child make his own bed—even if it's crooked—because he needs to conquer this skill. Perhaps you must tackle your worry over your fifth-grader's possible failure at school and let her do her own homework without your help. Face the snares in your life.

But don't stop there. Fight those snares. Free yourself both from them and from other traps you set for yourself.

Feather Your Nest

1. What snares you in the most unsuspecting moments of your day? How does your response to these temptations lead you to a "self" snare?

2. Can you remember a time when you successfully freed yourself from a struggle? How can what you learned in that instance help you today?

Prayer

Dear God, I feel trapped by _____. When I resist it, I find that I trap myself yet again with _____. Like a robin fighting his own reflection, I tend to fight myself when I try to change. Please help me to lay down my battle with myself. I invite you into this problem. Please, God, heal my heart and set me free.

Bird Fact

A BIRD'S EGG COMPRISES A WONDROUS BALANCE. IT
BEARS THE WEIGHT OF AN INCUBATING PARENT, AND
YET IS NOT SO THICK THAT THE GROWN HATCHLING
CANNOT GET OUT.

MARYJO KOCH, *BIRD EGG FEATHER NEST*

> "FOR I KNOW THE PLANS I HAVE FOR YOU," DECLARES
> THE LORD, "PLANS TO PROSPER YOU AND NOT TO HARM
> YOU, PLANS TO GIVE YOU A HOPE AND A FUTURE."
> —*JEREMIAH 29:11*

Make Room for God's Plans

Over the course of several years, a robin couple worked at building a nest in the small evergreen tree of my friend's yard. Each year a storm blew the nest from the tree, destroying the work of the birds and forcing them to build elsewhere. One year the robins built, my friend and her boys prayed, and the nest held. The mother robin laid her eggs and sat on them, only to have a whopper of a storm blow through my friend's neighborhood. But even though the nest was torn into halves, the mother still sat on her eggs in the upper half.

A few days after the storm, my friend reported that she had noticed a sparrow couple bringing moss and twigs to the evergreen. They were building their own nest in the bottom half of the robin's damaged nest! And the robin let them! Over the weeks that followed, the sparrows abandoned their work but the robins' eggs hatched.

How often we make our plans only to have the storms of life rearrange them. We wail, "No, God! Don't bring a storm!

I'll never survive it!" The storm comes, and our plans—maybe our nests—are damaged. We wonder how we'll recover. And then God brings a surprise. Perhaps it's someone to help us rebuild. Maybe it's a new perspective. Or it could be a complete shift in the direction we were heading.

How will we respond when God rearranges our plans? I confess that I'm not usually thrilled when God shifts what I so carefully put in place. I like life according to my specifications. And if a storm comes, I even prefer to rebuild according to my own desires. How about you?

Just as God promised the Israelites that their captivity would not last forever and that he had hopeful plans for their future, he longs to provide plans for our good. He uses the storms of our days to help us understand that he is bigger than our struggles and completely competent to overcome whatever trials we face.

When God allows a storm and then provides a solution to the damage it brings, will we receive it? Will we resist his ways because they are not ours? Or will we yield to his presence, even in our damaged nest?

Feather Your Nest

1. What storm are you currently encountering? How have you been damaged by it?

2. Are you open to God's solution for your situation? What do you need to adjust in order to receive his plans into your days?

Prayer

Dear God, I confess that I hate storms. I seem to prefer my solutions to yours. Please create an openness in me for your plans, your ways, your solutions. I believe you have my best interests in mind.

PART SEVEN

The View from the Nest

LOOKING TOWARD TOMORROW TODAY

There are only two lasting bequests
we can hope to give our children.
One of these is roots; the other, wings.
—HODDING CARTER III

Bird Fact

YOUNG BIRDS HATCH KNOWING A SORT OF GENERAL-
IZED SONG BUT MUST LISTEN TO ADULT BIRDS
SINGING IT "CORRECTLY," AND THEN IMITATE THEM,
BEFORE THEY PERFECT THEIR VOCAL TECHNIQUE.

CHRISTOPHER LEAHY,
IN *TREASURY OF NORTH AMERICAN BIRDLORE*

THESE COMMANDMENTS THAT I GIVE YOU TODAY ARE
TO BE UPON YOUR HEARTS. IMPRESS THEM ON YOUR
CHILDREN. TALK ABOUT THEM WHEN YOU SIT AT HOME
AND WHEN YOU WALK ALONG THE ROAD, WHEN YOU LIE
DOWN AND WHEN YOU GET UP. —DEUTERONOMY 6:6–7

Teach Your Children Well

No, Mommy, I want the *green* one!" three-year-old Eva
insisted. I looked at the row of plastic cups on the shelf.
Blue, yellow, red, even pink, but not a green one in sight.

"Eva, honey, we don't have a green cup. How about a red
or blue or yellow one?" I asked.

"Mommy, please can I have the *green* one?" Eva asked,
pointing clearly at the red cup.

I was confused. Eva was just learning her colors, but I had
thought she was a bit further along. Handing her the red cup,
I enunciated, "Eva, this *red*, not *green*."

She smiled, happy with her choice and oblivious to my
correction.

Later that afternoon we were reading books. I picked up
The Little Engine that Could. Eva pushed it aside and announced,
"No, Mommy, let's read the *green* one," pointing instead to
Goodnight Moon.

Eventually, I realized that when Eva said *green* she had actually meant *other*. At some time she must have heard me say, "Would you like the *green* one?" when the "other" choice really *was* green, and had consequently mixed up the two words in her vocabulary.

How closely our children observe us! And how readily they mimic our example—and not always in context!

Birds seem to naturally possess the ability to sing. Upon closer examination, the fact is that while baby birds sing rudimentary versions of their species' songs, unless they are exposed to live versions, their songs remain "baby songs." They need the example of their parents to learn to sing. Similarly, they need the example of their parents to feed themselves and fly.

What are your children learning from your example, Mom? Deuteronomy tells us to impart God's teaching to our children while we walk and sit down—in other words, all the time. While our children are born with a desire to know and love God, to use their talents in their world, and to invest in meaningful relationships, it is our job as moms to teach them *how*.

Feather Your Nest

1. Take an inventory of your child's behavior and characteristics. What can you identify that you have taught well?

2. In what areas can you more intentionally help your child grow by improving the example you provide? speech? manners? affection?

Prayer

Dear God, thank you for the areas in which I have taught my child well. Please show me where you want me to improve so that one day my child will be closer to who you want him to be.

Bird Fact

NATURE PLACES STRINGENT REQUIREMENTS ON THE
MECHANICS OF FLIGHT. TOO MUCH WEIGHT, TOO LIT-
TLE PHYSICAL STRENGTH, TOO LOW A METABOLISM,
AND THE BIRD NEVER LEAVES THE GROUND.

MARYJO KOCH, *BIRD EGG FEATHER NEST*

> *B*UT THOSE WHO HOPE IN THE LORD WILL RENEW
> THEIR STRENGTH. THEY WILL SOAR ON WINGS LIKE
> EAGLES; THEY WILL RUN AND NOT GROW WEARY, THEY
> WILL WALK AND NOT BE FAINT.   —*ISAIAH 40:31*

Remember Your Goal as a Mom

*I*t's been two years now. For the first twelve years of her life, Eva was "put down" at bedtime. Her father and I took turns each evening saying prayers, tucking her in, kissing her goodnight, turning out her light. And then two years ago she met me in the hall and announced, "I can put myself down, Mom. I know how to pray."

Of course, I was stunned. I'd endured the moment she pushed the bottle away from her lips. I hadn't walked her to school for years. I'd long since given up picking out her clothes. But to not put her down?

A mother eagle prepares her babies to leave the nest by unfluffing it. With her beak, she tugs out all the downy, soft stuff that has made such a cozy bed and sends it floating over the side until only thorny, prickly sticks remain. Who would want to stay in such a nest?

In my life, it is more often my child who does the "unfluffing," and if I'm wise, I pick up the cues and follow along. Moments like Eva's decision that she didn't need to be "put down" are monuments of perspective in my life. They direct my gaze away from the everyday chores of mothering and refocus me on my goal. What am I up to in my mothering, anyway? What is the goal of the laundry, the meals, the lectures, the homework monitoring, the carpooling?

The goal of mothering is to get the babies out of the nest and flying on their own. The goal is to see them soar on wings like eagles.

Whether the unfluffing comes by their beaks or my own, I am learning to welcome it as it reminds me of what I'm about in this nest-building calling after all. We build a nest to hatch our young and, eventually, we empty the nest of them as we watch them fly.

Feather Your Nest

1. Who does the unfluffing in your relationship with your child? Why do you think this is the case?

2. How is God asking you to respond to this challenge of unfluffing? Can you specifically state and embrace your goal for mothering?

Prayer

Dear God, help me understand that my goal as a mother is to raise a child to independence from me and dependence on you. Give me the courage to cooperate with the unfluffing process, even when I would rather stay cozy in the soft places of my nest.

Bird Fact

YOUNG THAT HAVE LEFT THE NEST BUT ARE STILL FED
BY THE PARENTS ARE CALLED FLEDGLINGS. THIS STAGE
LASTS SEVERAL WEEKS OR MORE, DEPENDING ON THE
SPECIES. . . . THE FLEDGLINGS GENERALLY DO NOT GO
BACK INTO THE BOX ONCE THEY LEAVE, BUT WANDER
ABOUT A GREAT DEAL; THEY MAY MOVE OUT OF YOUR
YARD.

DONALD AND LILLLIAN STOKES,
THE COMPLETE BIRDHOUSE BOOK

> THERE IS A TIME FOR EVERYTHING, AND A SEASON FOR
> EVERY ACTIVITY UNDER HEAVEN.   —*ECCLESIASTES 3:1*

Practice Today for Tomorrow

As I drove through my neighborhood, my eye spied a wad of sticks stuck high up in the naked branches of a cottonwood tree. An empty nest. It was February, and in Denver no buds—much less leaves—appear until at least April. The sparse months of late fall and winter reveal the skeletons of trees and the leftover nests from previous years.

Against the startling blue sky of a clear winter day, the nest flew like a flag, proclaiming to me as I drove by, "There is a time for everything, and a season for every activity under heaven." A time for building a nest. A time for feeding the young within its folds. And a time for nudging them out.

That nudging out part always seemed so far away in my early years of mothering. My attention was on the basics of stuffing my babies' beaks with food, keeping the nest clean, and responding to my mate while the babies beckoned. But as the years have passed, the empty nest is more and more a part of my life, and I'm discovering that God gives me practice sessions today for the empty nest of tomorrow.

Ethan is invited on a camping trip with another family for a whole weekend. Late at night, I pause at his bedroom door, view the debris of his preparations, and feel the absence of his presence. I am happy for him. He is growing and full and free. But I can touch the hole created by his departure and carry it forward into the future, when it will last longer. In the emptiness of his room, I am practicing for the empty nest.

Eva leaves for camp for two weeks. Her bed stays made. Her curlers sit on the bathroom counter, cool and unused. I am not called to wind her hair around them. I do her chores: feeding the cat, emptying the dishwasher. I take messages from her friends who call and give out her camp address for them to write her there. There are only three places at the table. I sit on her bed and practice her absence from my nest.

These moments used to shock me, but no longer. I have come to expect them and invest myself fully in using them for the purpose I believe God has given them. *There is a time for everything, and a season for every activity under heaven.* Today I am practicing for tomorrow. Are you?

Feather Your Nest

1. As your children grow and change, can you find times to touch their transitions? How have they moved from dependence to independence?

2. How can you practice today for the empty nest of tomorrow?

Prayer

Dear God, while it grieves my heart in some spots, the thought of an empty nest also warms it. I know that your plan is for me to teach my children to fly alone with you. Give me the courage to practice today for tomorrow.

Bird Fact

MIGRATION IS FREQUENTLY A DANGEROUS, EXHAUST-
ING, AND FATAL ORDEAL. AND YET THE IMPULSE TO
MIGRATE IS SO DEEPLY INGRAINED THAT EVEN SOME
BIRDS IN CAGES——WELL-FED AND CARED FOR——EXPE-
RIENCE "MIGRATORY FEVER" AT THE TIMES OF YEAR
WHEN THEIR FREE RELATIVES NORMALLY TAKE WING.

MARYJO KOCH, *BIRD EGG FEATHER NEST*

*I*F ANYONE WOULD COME AFTER ME, HE MUST DENY
HIMSELF AND TAKE UP HIS CROSS DAILY AND FOLLOW ME.
—*LUKE 9:23*

Migration Time

As Eva approached her thirteenth birthday, she began to hint at her desire to redo her bedroom. The pale blue walls were muraled with a picket fence and flowers. A tiny sparrow, wings freely spread, flew in the clouds above the fence. Her white iron daybed was covered with an eyelet comforter, and her clothes were stuffed into a white dresser. She said she wanted something more grown-up.

Understanding her desire and its symbolism, her dad and I agreed. We spent a weekend shopping for furniture. She received a new comforter splashed with brighter, more sophisticated colors for a birthday present.

Several days before her new bed was to be delivered, a few of her friends came over for a painting party. Eva had chosen cream paint. Very simple. Nothing fussy.

I stood in the doorway and watched the picket fence and blue sky eaten up by sweeps of cream paint. The room looked bigger, cleaner, a new palette for Eva's posters. I could picture the thumbtack pierces of the future.

As Eva rounded the corner of her room to the last wall, she came eyeball to eyeball with the sparrow. She paused. Lifting the roller, she started to paint, then paused again. Turning to me, her forehead creased, she asked, "Mom, could you paint around the bird for me? I want to save it."

Today the sparrow still flies, wings freely spread, on Eva's wall. As my daughter bumps up against the edges of our home nest, explores her relationship with God for herself, and considers how to follow after him in her days, the sparrow reminds us all that she is learning to fly solo.

It also reminds me that while I hope our own migratory paths will lead to the same destination—a closer relationship with God—they may not follow the same route. I am to pick up my cross and follow Jesus daily. And so is she.

How challenging it is as mothers to truly comprehend this truth! We're the ones who bend to tie our children's shoes so they won't trip along the way. We select balanced diets, make sure they get enough sleep, supervise homework, and insist on good manners. We provide all that is necessary for their journey. And then they fly off alone to God's appointed place.

And we, Mom, pick up our own cross and continue on, following after the one who is leading us to where he wants us to go.

Feather Your Nast

1. Does your child know Jesus as his or her personal Savior? Is it time for you to introduce Jesus to your child and to begin the teaching of how to follow him, no matter where he leads in life?

2. How does your path differ from your child's? In what ways is God leading you to follow him with words that are for you only?

Prayer

Dear God, help my child grow in her relationship with you so that as you lead, she will follow. And God, I pray the same for me. Help me to follow you wherever you lead.

Bird Fact

SOMETIMES THE PARENTS MUST PERSUADE A BABY

BIRD TO LEAVE, PERHAPS REFUSING TO FEED HIM SO

THAT HE WILL VENTURE OUT FOR DINNER.

ALEXANDER WETMORE,
SONG AND GARDEN BIRDS OF NORTH AMERICA

*H*E TOLD THEM ANOTHER PARABLE: "THE KINGDOM
OF HEAVEN IS LIKE A MUSTARD SEED, WHICH A MAN
TOOK AND PLANTED IN HIS FIELD. THOUGH IT IS THE
SMALLEST OF ALL YOUR SEEDS, YET WHEN IT GROWS, IT IS
THE LARGEST OF GARDEN PLANTS AND BECOMES A TREE,
SO THAT THE BIRDS OF THE AIR COME AND PERCH IN ITS
BRANCHES." —*MATTHEW 13:31–32*

The Impact of Today on Tomorrow

*I*t's easy to believe that what we do as moms makes little
difference. Wiping counters, noses, and bottoms—they are
such *small* things. And yet mothering today impacts tomorrow
for eternity.

Jesus compares the kingdom of heaven to a mustard
seed—the smallest seed known in biblical times, yet one that
grew into one of the largest garden plants. A mustard seed grew
into a mustard tree, where all the birds of the air could perch
in its branches. In the book of Mark, we're told that all the birds
of the air can "perch in its shade." A huge resting, nesting spot
from a tiny seed!

Such is mothering—and such is MOPS. MOPS stands for
Mothers of Preschoolers. It's an international support organization for moms focused primarily on nurturing moms so that

they can be better moms. It started small, a few moms meeting together, planting the seed of their vision. Decades later, MOPS is big enough for all the moms of the world to rest and nest in during the season of mothering young children.

At MOPS, as in mothering, small things do matter. Whenever you struggle to validate your significance in this nesting season, look to MOPS and to the mustard seed for a reminder.

Mothering is a small seed that grows into a large plant. Today, as you correct and praise, as you guide and direct, as you warn and follow through, remember the impact today has on tomorrow. It may seem your efforts are sooooo small. But great is the impact of something small as it is pressed into the soil of a child's life and nurtured over time.

Feather Your Nest

1. What specific seed are you pressing today into the soil of your child's life? Even though it seems small, what is the potential impact of this investment in the life of your child?

2. How has God invested similarly in your life? What small investment was made by your mother or father or teacher that today has yielded great rewards?

Prayer

Dear God, convince me that my small investment today will yield a great impact tomorrow. Give me the perspective I need in order to continue even when I feel so insignificant.

Afterword

bird's nest is a nest for a season. It is built and utilized for the explicit purpose of hatching and raising her young. The female bird does not *live* in her nest for all of her life.

We women do. In the days before marriage and children, we nest. During the season of raising our young, we increase our focus on the nest. And following our children's departure from the nest, we cope with its emptiness and learn to reinhabit a place that has changed in its most basic of functions.

Throughout all our ages and stages, our seasons as daughters, wives, mothers, and women, we are wise to remember the lesson of the sparrow and the swallow: the building of our nests directly in God's presence, in a place near his altar. As illustrated in these meditations, in early motherhood days, our moments with God come mainly in quick gulps. We do well to realize that these "quick gulps" are not the sum total of our days with him. Eventually, we will have the time and energy to focus more deeply. In short, Mom, make it your practice to *graze* on the fast food of God's presence during those days you are mothering young children. But prepare yourself to take advantage of the time when your children are otherwise occupied and learn to *dine* deeply with God as well.

God meets us as moms in all seasons of our days. Rest comes when we learn to meet him there as well—in a nest, near his altar.

MOPS IS...

MOPS stands for Mothers of Preschoolers, a program designed for mothers with children under school age. These women come from different backgrounds and lifestyles, yet have similar needs and a shared desire to be the best mothers they can be!

A MOPS group provides a caring, accepting atmosphere for today's mother of preschoolers. Here she has an opportunity to share concerns, explore areas of creativity and hear instruction that equips her for the responsibilities of family and community. The MOPS program also includes MOPPETS, a loving, learning experience for children.

Approximately 2,000 groups meet in churches throughout the United States, Canada, and 11 other countries, to meet the needs of more than 80,000 women. Many more mothers are encouraged by the media arms of MOPS: *MomSense* radio and newsletter, MOPS' web site, and publications such as this book.

To find out if there is a MOPS group near you, or if you're interested in general information regarding MOPS, please write or call: MOPS International, PO Box 102200, Denver, CO 80250-2200. Phone: 303-733-5353 or 1-800-929-1287. Fax: 303-733-5770. E-mail: Info@MOPS.org. Web site: http://www.MOPS.org. To learn how to start a MOPS group, call 1-888-910-MOPS. For MOPS products call The MOPS Shop at 1-888-545-4040.

Source Books

Boring, Mel. *Birds, Nests and Eggs.* Minnetonka, MN: Northwood Press, 1996.

Eriksson, Paul S. and Alan Pistorius, eds. *Treasury of North American Birdlore.* Middlebury, VT: Paul S. Eriksson Publisher, 1987.

Koch, Maryjo. *Bird Egg Feather Nest.* San Francisco: Collins Publishers, Swans Islands Books, 1994.

Stokes, Donald and Lillian Stokes. *The Complete Birdhouse Book.* Boston, MA: Little, Brown and Company, 1990.

Wangerin, Walt. The Manger is Empty. Grand Rapids: Zondervan, 199?.

Wetmore, Alexander. *Song and Garden Birds of North America.* Washington D. C.: National Geographic Society, 1963.

Also Available from MOPS

Beyond Macaroni and Cheese (*Lagerborg & Parks*)
Chronicles of Childhood (*Morgan*)
A Cure for the Growly Bugs (*Lagerborg*)
Getting Out of Your Kids' Faces (*Bell*)
Learning to Let Go (*Kuykendall*)
Mommy, I Love You Just Because . . .
Mom's Devotional Bible
Mom to Mom (*Morgan*)
Mom to Mom, audio (*Morgan*)
A Mother's Footprints of Faith (*Kuykendall*)
A Mother's Touch
Raising Great Kids (*Cloud / Townsend*)
What Every Child Needs (*Morgan & Kuykendall*)
What Every Child Needs, audio (*Morgan & Kuykendall*)
What Every Mom Needs (*Morgan & Kuykendall*)
What Every Mom Needs, audio (*Morgan & Kuykendall*)